DEEP DIVE

A LEGO® ADVENTURE IN THE REAL WORLD

by Penelope Arlon
and Tory Gordon-Harris

You won't believe how many stunning creatures there are in the sea!

SCHOLASTIC

New York   Toronto   London   Auckland
Sydney   Mexico City   New Delhi   Hong Kong

Welcome, LEGO fans!

LEGO® Minifigures show you the world in a unique nonfiction program.

This leveled reader is part of a program of LEGO® nonfiction books, with something for all the family, at every age and stage. LEGO nonfiction books have amazing facts, beautiful real-world photos, and minifigures everywhere, leading the fun and discovery.

To find out about the books in the program, visit www.scholastic.com.

Leveled readers from Scholastic are designed to support your child's efforts to learn how to read at every age and stage.

LEVEL 1 READER

Beginning reader
Preschool–Grade 1
Sight words
Words to sound out
Simple sentences

LEVEL 2 READER

Developing reader
Grades 1–2
New vocabulary
Longer sentences

LEVEL 3 READER

Growing reader
Grades 1–3
Reading for inspiration
and information

Contents

BUILD IT!

Check out the epic building ideas when you see me!

Come on an incredible undersea adventure. There's so much to see in the sea.

I might just explore from inside this sub. It looks a bit fishy out there.

Dive deep!

We have better maps of the surface of Mars than of our ocean. Dive in! There is so much to explore. Almost three-quarters of our Earth is covered in ocean. Some parts are 7 miles (11 km) deep. The ocean is filled with amazing creatures.

Let's go! There are more than a million plants and animals in the ocean. I want to see a shark!

I'm after a shipwreck and a ton of treasure!

Hope you spot some amazing fish. Catch you later!

But watch out, divers. Some are dangerous. Look out! Shark fin! This is going to be a wild adventure!

BUILD IT!

Build the best-ever submarine to explore the ocean.

Hey, King! Make me a huge wave to carry me through the book!

Don't find yourself in deep water!

Let's hope that these divers don't get into any hot water. I'll be watching.

Coral reef

Did you know? A third of all fish live in coral reefs.

Can you see that flash of pink? Only a few yards below the waves is a world of color. Coral reefs are the largest living things on our planet. They look like rock, but they are made up of tiny sea creatures. Coral is alive! Coral reefs are home to more

HEARD THIS WORD?

shoal: a large group of fish

Whoa! Have you lost your brain?

No, silly! That brain-shaped rock is actually coral!

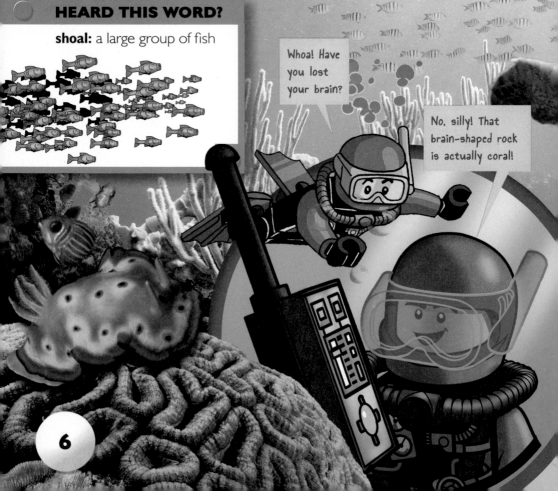

sea life than anywhere else in the ocean. That flash of pink is a shoal of fish. Find a purple-spotted sea slug. Watch a turtle swim by with flapping fins.

BUILD IT!

The divers really need an underwater exploration station. Fill it up with cool tools for exploring.

- What is the strongest creature in the sea?
- A mussel!

7

It's eat or be eaten on the reef. Dull colors help animals hide. Bright colors can show that a creature is poisonous. The colors yell, "Don't eat me!" Animals also take care in other ways. The puffer fish can blow itself up to twice its original size.

Down here, there are a few rules. You can look at the animals, but remember the rule about no touching. Got it?

Look at that awesome octopus. Ahh, it wants a huge, eight-armed hug!

Watch out! Some octopus bites can kill in minutes! That octopus is armed, fully armed!

The most important thing to remember in the sea is DON'T TOUCH ANYTHING.

Are sea animals more colorful than land animals?

Puffer fish blow up and pop out their spines.

The blue-ringed octopus is one of the most poisonous animals in the whole ocean.

This is creepy. I feel like I'm being followed . . .

• What did the seaweed say when it was stuck to the bottom of the sea?
• Kelp, kelp!

Swim away from the reef into an underwater forest. Keep still, and the forest comes to life. Giant seaweeds, called kelp, grow on the seafloor. They grow all the way up to the water's surface. Splash! A seal dives down to search for a tasty meal. The fish swim into the shady weeds to hide. The spiky sea urchins keep safe. They are too prickly to eat!

BUILD IT!

Build an underwater forest for your divers to hide in.

This is one strange forest. Kelp can grow to 150 feet (46 m). I'm glad that I don't have to chop this down!

11

Sailfish sometimes leap out of the water. Woo-hoo, we're both catching waves!

Open ocean

Far from the beach, there are thousands of miles of open ocean. Fish swim in huge shoals. Sailfish are the fastest predators in the ocean. A team of sailfish swims around a shoal of sardines. The sardines swim into a tight ball. They swim close to keep safe.

But the sailfish are not the kings of the ocean. The great white shark shoots upward. Its massive mouth is open wide. The sailfish flee. The shark can smell blood from 3 miles (5 km) away. It speeds toward its prey at 15 miles per hour (24 kph). One bite of its 300 teeth, and the sardines are lunch.

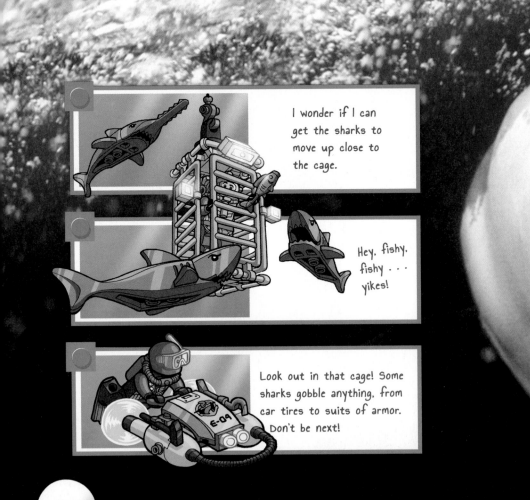

I wonder if I can get the sharks to move up close to the cage.

Hey, fishy, fishy . . . yikes!

Look out in that cage! Some sharks gobble anything, from car tires to suits of armor. Don't be next!

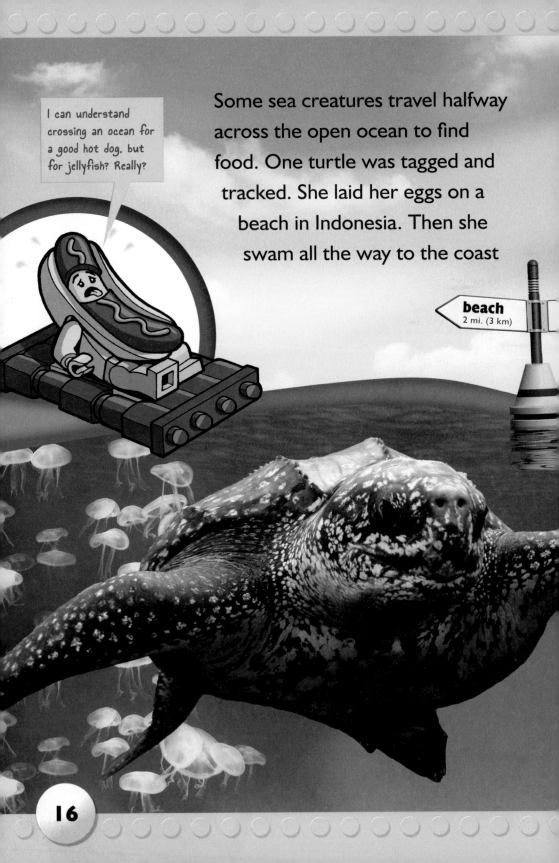

Some sea creatures travel halfway across the open ocean to find food. One turtle was tagged and tracked. She laid her eggs on a beach in Indonesia. Then she swam all the way to the coast

I can understand crossing an ocean for a good hot dog, but for jellyfish? Really?

beach
2 mi. (3 km)

of Oregon, in the United States. She traveled 12,774 miles (20,558 km). She crossed the whole Pacific Ocean to find jellyfish—her favorite snack!

jellies
12,772 mi. (20,555 km)

BUILD IT!

Build a turtle strong enough to swim across the ocean.

I've been following this reptile for days. I'm seasick of this now. Are we there yet?

Sigh . . . another 10,000 miles (16,090 km) to go. I'll be on this ship for over a year!

Leatherback turtles flap their flippers like birds flap their wings, to "fly" through the water.

Check out these
ocean giants. The whale
shark is the biggest fish in the world. It's
as long as a bus. But it doesn't eat anything
larger than your littlest fingernail! A lion's
mane jellyfish has tentacles that are longer
than a blue whale. Imagine seeing a shoal of
manta rays as big as small
planes flapping past.

The whale shark swims with its mouth open,
scooping up tiny plants and animals to eat.
Jaw-dropping!

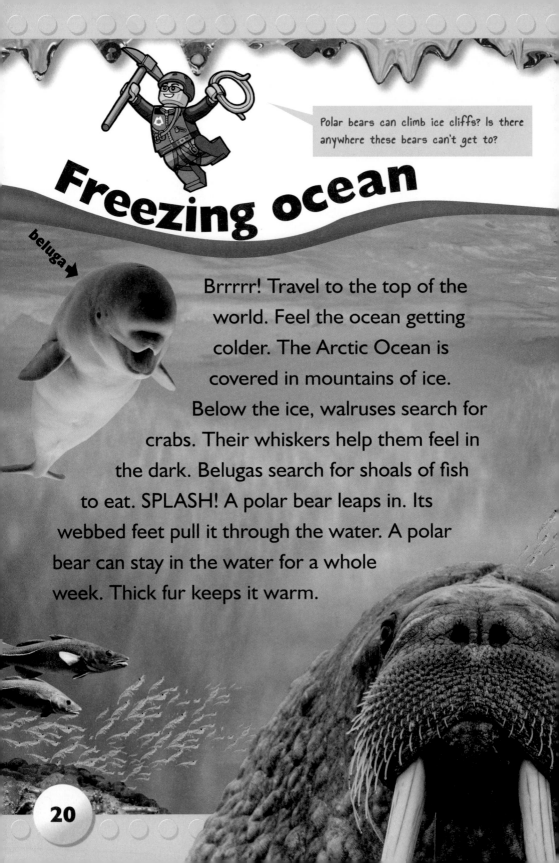

Polar bears can climb ice cliffs? Is there anywhere these bears can't get to?

Freezing ocean

beluga

Brrrrr! Travel to the top of the world. Feel the ocean getting colder. The Arctic Ocean is covered in mountains of ice. Below the ice, walruses search for crabs. Their whiskers help them feel in the dark. Belugas search for shoals of fish to eat. SPLASH! A polar bear leaps in. Its webbed feet pull it through the water. A polar bear can stay in the water for a whole week. Thick fur keeps it warm.

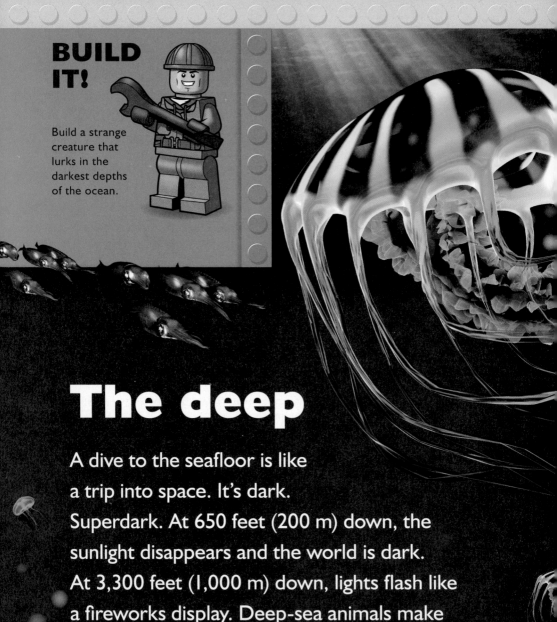

BUILD IT!

Build a strange creature that lurks in the darkest depths of the ocean.

The deep

A dive to the seafloor is like a trip into space. It's dark. Superdark. At 650 feet (200 m) down, the sunlight disappears and the world is dark. At 3,300 feet (1,000 m) down, lights flash like a fireworks display. Deep-sea animals make light in their bodies and use it to talk. Some use light as a warning. Others use it to find friends in the dark. Some shrimp spit out light to confuse predators!

Humans know more about the surface of the Moon than the bottom of the ocean.

Arrgh! It's a glow-in-the-dark shark! The lantern shark lights up to warn predators to keep away.

Are you kidding me? There are sharks down here, too? Lights off, buddy. We're trying to explore.

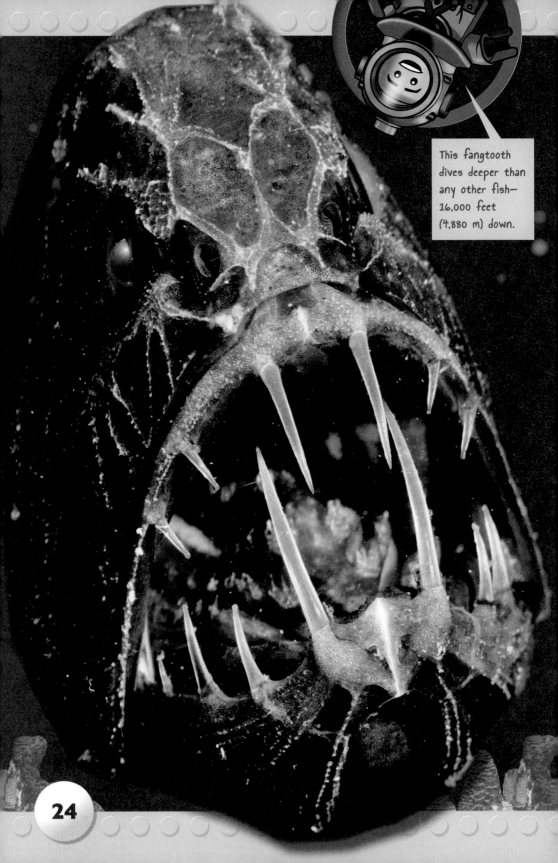

This fangtooth dives deeper than any other fish—16,000 feet (4,880 m) down.

The creatures of the deep are very strange. It's like they just swam out of a scary movie! Hairy crabs and huge clams live by underwater chimneys that spit out hot liquid. The fangtooth can't shut its mouth like we can—its teeth are too long! The dumbo octopus is as big as a beach ball. Those things sticking out of its head are fins, not ears. It's out of this world down in the deep.

dumbo octopus ➤

Careful, dude, that sizzling-hot seawater can get up to 700°F (370°C).

We don't want to get into hot water. Let's go.

Shipwreck!

HEARD THIS WORD?

shipwreck: the remains of a ship that has sunk or been destroyed at sea

Before there were airplanes, more things were taken across the ocean by ship. But there were dangers at sea. Greedy pirates searched the seas, stealing ships and their

Whoa! Some of the wrecks down here are hundreds of years old!

That doesn't mean that I'm not still around to protect my treasure!

Fa la la. In the past, sailors believed that if they heard a mermaid's song, the ship would sink. Oops!

BUILD IT!

Build a ship, but make it look as if it has been sitting at the bottom of the ocean for 100 years!

treasures. Every so often, ships were wrecked on rocks or icebergs. Others were destroyed by storms or fire. There may be as many as 3 million shipwrecks lying on the ocean floor.

Shiver me timbers! There's a shipwreck! Let's find the treasure. Unless someone else has gotten there first. Ships that sank took their treasures with them. Find a sunken pirate ship, and it may be filled with stolen jewels, gold, and coins. There are hundreds of wrecks still to be found. It's the world's biggest treasure hunt!

If you find a wreck, and there isn't an owner looking for it, you can keep the loot. This treasure is mine!

I saw it first. Let's share it!

Build a LEGO® reef!

It's a minifigure adventure in the ocean! Fill the coral reef with your colorful stickers. Who is the shark sneaking up on? Make sure that your divers can escape from any danger!

Amazing ocean words

armor
A metal covering worn to protect the body in battle.

bill
An animal's hard, pointy jaws.

dinosaur
A reptile, often very large, with four legs and scaly or feathered skin. Dinosaurs died out 65 million years ago.

jellyfish
A sea creature with a soft, see-through body and long tentacles.

kelp
A large brown plant that grows in the sea.

mussel
A sea animal that lives in a long black shell.

pirate
A person who attacks and steals ships at sea.

poisonous
Capable of causing sickness or death.

predator
An animal that hunts and eats other animals.

prey
An animal that is hunted and eaten by another animal.

reptile
An animal with scaly skin that lays eggs. Turtles are reptiles.

shipwreck
The remains of a ship that has sunk or been destroyed at sea.

shoal
A large group of fish.

shrimp
A small sea animal with a shell and a long tail.

tentacle
An animal's long, thin body part, used for movement and for feeling and holding things. Jellyfish have tentacles.

Help! I'm done down here. Get me back to dry land before I see that pesky shark again . . .

Index

Credits

For the LEGO Group: Randi Kirsten Sørensen *Assistant Manager*; Peter Moorby *Licensing Coordinator*; Heidi K. Jensen *Licensing Manager*; Paul Hansford *Creative Publishing Manager*; Martin Leighton Lindhardt *Publishing Graphic Designer*

Photographs ©: cover shark: Masterfile; cover reef: fox17/Fotolia; cover clown fish: Kletr/Fotolia; cover seahorse: MagicColors/iStockphoto; cover sea turtle: M. Swiet Productions/Getty Images; cover water background: peangdao/iStockphoto; cover all other fish: mirecca/iStockphoto; back cover octopus: Jonmilnes/Dreamstime; back cover water background: peangdao/iStockphoto; 1 fish: Rich Carey/Shutterstock, Inc.; 1 background: Natalia Lyubetskaya/iStockphoto; 2 sea turtle: M. Swiet Productions/Getty Images; 3 center left fish: KITTIPONG KHUMBOON/Shutterstock, Inc.; 3 center right fish: ArtPhaneuf/iStockphoto; 4 center left foreground fish: strmko/iStockphoto; 4 center left background fish: Rich Carey/Shutterstock, Inc.; 4 center right fish: David Carbo/Shutterstock, Inc.; 4-5 bottom background: yannp/iStockphoto; 4-5 top background: Pakhnyushchy/Shutterstock, Inc.; 5 top fin: adventtr/iStockphoto; 5 center background: Rich Carey/Shutterstock, Inc.; 5 center foreground: Vlad61/Shutterstock, Inc.; 6 water background: Justin Lewis/Getty Images; 6 center left: Kim Briers/Shutterstock, Inc.; 6 bottom left yellow fish: Howard Chew/iStockphoto; 6 bottom left: Aqua Images/Shutterstock, Inc.; 6 center right fish: Jung Hsuan/Shutterstock, Inc.; 6 lion fish: LauraD/Shutterstock, Inc.; 7 right reef: Anastasia Markus/Shutterstock, Inc.; 7 sea turtle: M. Swiet Productions/Getty Images; 7 bottom yellow fish: sserg_dibrova/iStockphoto/Thinkstock; 7 bottom orange fish: Rich Carey/Shutterstock, Inc.; 7 water background: Justin Lewis/Getty Images; 8 center right fish: GlobalP/iStockphoto; 8-9 top background: iiasbgun/yannp/iStockphoto; 8-9 bottom background: stephankerkhofs/iStockphoto; 9 bottom octopus: Jman78/iStockphoto; 9 starfish: blackwaterimages/iStockphoto; 9 top octopus: Divography/iStockphoto; 10 bottom left fish: ArtPhaneuf/iStockphoto; 10 bottom right urchin: atanasovski/iStockphoto; 10-11 background: fdastudillo/iStockphoto; 11 sea lion: beusbeus/iStockphoto; 11 bottom right kelp: Ethan Daniels/Shutterstock, Inc.; 12 sailfish: Jesse Cancelmo/Alamy Images; 12-13 top background: Davide_Lorpesti/iStockphoto; 12-13 bottom background: ifiashgun/yannp/iStockphoto; 14-15 background: Barcroft/Getty Images; 16 turtle: Michael Patrick O'Neill/Science Source; 16 buoy: archideaphoto/iStockphoto; 16-17 top background: fazoni/iStockphoto; 16-17 bottom background: yannp/iStockphoto; 16-17 jellyfish: ivylingpy/iStockphoto; 18-19 whale shark: Predrag Vuckovic/iStockphoto; 18-19 background, manta ray: Annetje/Shutterstock, Inc.; 19 diver: MaFelipe/iStockphoto; 19 jellyfish: Jan-Dirk Hansen/Alamy Images; 20 beluga whale: CostinT/iStockphoto; 20 crab: Kari Kolehmainen/Shutterstock, Inc.; 20-21 top icicles: Merzavka/iStockphoto; 20-21 walrus: mikeuk/iStockphoto; 20-21 background, polar bear: fotokon/iStockphoto; 20-21 krill: pilipenkoD/iStockphoto; 20-21 fish: Vlada Zhi/Shutterstock, Inc.; 21 top right: jrphoto6/iStockphoto; 22 top blue jellyfish: nutthaphol/iStockphoto; 22 bottom blue jellyfish: nutthaphol/iStockphoto; 22-23 yellow blue jellyfish: CoreyFord/iStockphoto; 22-23 squids: Tracey Winholt/Shutterstock, Inc.; 22-23 background: rustycloud/iStockphoto; 23 purple jellyfish: evantravels/Shutterstock, Inc.; 24 main: Dante Fenolio/Science Source; 24 sea vents: B. Murton/Southampton Oceanography Centre/Science Source; 25 center right: Dante Fenolio/Science Source; 25 top right: Dante Fenolio/Science Source; 25 smoke: LuVo/iStockphoto; 25 sea vents: B. Murton/Southampton Oceanography Centre/Science Source; 26 top left fish: Lisa-Blue/iStockphoto; 26-27 background: Predrag Vuckovic/iStockphoto; 27 center right: WhitcombeRD/iStockphoto; 27 center left fish: Jung Hsuan/Shutterstock, Inc.; 27 bottom wreck: Adnan Buyuk/Shutterstock, Inc.; 27 bottom fish: sserg_dibrova/iStockphoto/Thinkstock; 28 treasure chest: Dim Dimich/Shutterstock, Inc.; 28 shark: StevenBenjamin/iStockphoto; 28-29 background: rangzzz/Shutterstock, Inc.; 28-29 school of fish: Leonardo Gonzalez/Shutterstock, Inc.; 28-29 bottom reef: Richard Whitcombe/Shutterstock, Inc.; 28-29 wreck: Shane Gross/Shutterstock, Inc.; 29 bottom pink coral: mehmettorlak/iStockphoto; 29 treasure chest: dblight/iStockphoto; 29 bottom right reef: Vlad61/Shutterstock, Inc.; 30 left reef: desertdiver/iStockphoto; 30 top left fish: strmko/iStockphoto; 30 bottom left fish: Rich Carey/Shutterstock, Inc.; 30 left blue fish: mirecca/iStockphoto; 30 seahorse: MagicColors/iStockphoto; 30-31 background: Natalia Lyubetskaya/iStockphoto; 30-31 school of fish: Jung Hsuan/Shutterstock, Inc.; 31 striped fish: marno31/iStockphoto; 31 bottom reef: IBorisoff/iStockphoto; 31 yellow fish: sserg_dibrova/iStockphoto/Thinkstock; 32 background: untouchablephoto/iStockphoto.

All LEGO® illustrations and stickers by Paul Lee and Sean Wang.

Thanks to the pirates for leaving us the treasure. And thanks to the shark for not getting the munchies!

ISBN 978-0-545-94770-1

10 9 8 7 6 5 4 3 2 1   16 17 18 19 20

Printed in the U.S.A. 40
First edition, July 2016

ISBN: S-TK5-94770-7   PO# 512478